DATE DUE

JUL 1 1996		JUL 5 2001	
NOV 8 1996		AUG 28 2001	
JUL 21 1997 NOV 6 1997		JUL 1 2003	
AUG 25 1998 DEC 23 1998		APR 15 2004 JUL 20 2004	
MAR 16 1999		JUL 29 2005 3/5/07 wBZZZ MAY 25 2007	
APR 23 1999		APR 30 2009	
AUG 26 1999		JUN 17 2013 JUN 06 2014	
DEC 21 1999 DEC 5 2000 APR 24 2001		MAY 5 2016 MAY 20 2016	

BUTTERFLIES

designed and written by Althea
illustrated by the author
and Maureen Galvani

Longman Group USA Inc.

Published in the United States of America by Longman Group USA Inc.
© 1977, 1988 Althea Braithwaite

Originally published in Great Britain in a slightly altered form by Longman Group UK Limited

ISBN: 0-88462-180-4   (library bound)
ISBN: 0-88462-181-2   (paperback)

Printed in the United States of America

88 89 90 10 9 8 7 6 5 4 3 2 1

Library of Congress Cataloging-in-Publication Data

Althea.
  Butterflies / designed and written by Althea ; illustrated by the author and Maureen Galvani.
    p. cm.--(Life-cycle books / Althea)
    Summary: Describes the appearance, reproduction, and life cycle of the butterfly.
    1. Butterflies--Juvenile literature. [1. Butterflies] I. Galvani, Maureen, ill. II. Ti-
tle. III. Series: Althea. Life-cycle books.
QL544.2.A47   1988
599.78'9--dc   88-8506
ISBN 0-88462-180-4   CIP
ISBN 0-88462-181-2 (pbk.)   AC

Notes for parents and teachers

Life-Cycle Books have been specially written and designed as a simple, yet informative, series of factual nature books for young children.

The illustrations are bright and clear, and children can "read" the pictures while the story is read to them.

The text has been specially set in large type to make it easy for children to follow along or even to read for themselves.

It is summer.
The sun is shining.
Flowers are in bloom.
Butterflies are fluttering
together in the sky.

They mate, and the female
butterfly lays her eggs
on the leaves of a plant.
She lays a hundred or so
eggs in hidden places.
Then she flies away.

Many eggs will get eaten,
but some remain safe.
After a few days,
tiny caterpillars eat their
way out of these eggs.

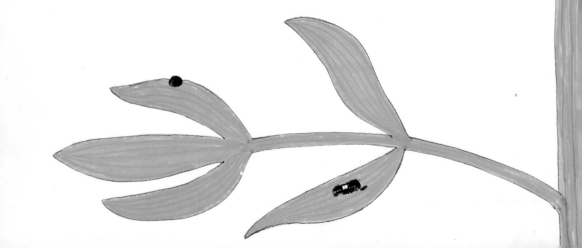

The little caterpillars are
very hungry.
First they eat their eggshells
and then they begin to eat
the plant's leaves.

With six front legs and
ten back legs, a caterpillar
can cling safely to a leaf.
It eats and eats.
As it grows bigger
its skin splits open
and it crawls out
wearing a new skin.

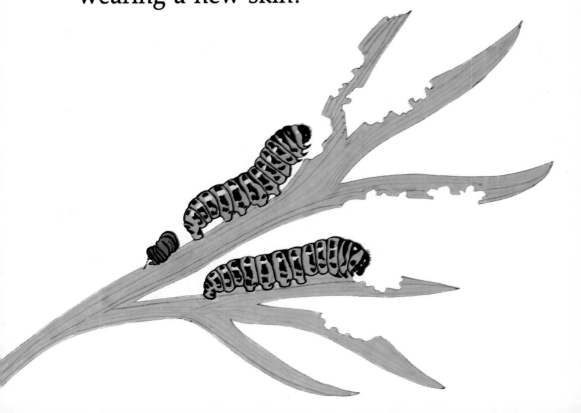

This happens many times.
Each time a caterpillar crawls
out of an old skin, it looks
more colorful than it did before.
The new skin is larger, too.
There is more room to grow.

Color protects caterpillars
from some enemies.
A green caterpillar is safer if
it looks like a leaf or stalk.
Spots on its head look like big
eyes and birds are scared off.

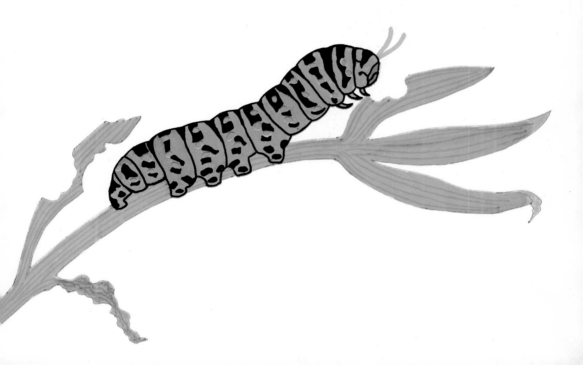

The caterpillar eats many leaves
and grows very big.
It makes a silken thread and
ties itself to the stalk of a plant.
A new change is going to begin.
Its skin splits for the last time.

The caterpillar is now
a chrysalis.
A hard shell covers
its body.
It cannot move or
eat and remains
attached to the stalk.

Winter comes.
The plant dies, but still
the hard shell of the chrysalis
remains, protecting the butterfly
that is forming inside.

When spring arrives
plants begin to grow again.

The sun shines and
warms the chrysalis.
Slowly, very slowly,
the outside cracks open.

The new and beautiful butterfly
crawls out.
It spreads its wings
to dry in the sunshine.

The butterfly flutters away
to search for nectar in the flowers
and to find other butterflies
just like itself.

Summer is here again.

SWALLOWTAIL butterflies are relatively common and easy to recognize by the tips on the second pair of wings. The yellow-and-black swallowtails are only one variation; others are blue, black or even white.

Butterflies are insects and their development is in four stages: egg, caterpillar (larva), chrysalis (pupa) and adult. This growth is pictured here, sometimes with enlargement for clarity. Because a butterfly's life is so closely related to flowering plants, it's interesting to see how the plants shown from page to page help track the time from one summer to the next. The flowers bloom, fade and die, to be replaced by the blossoms of the next summer.

Once the female butterfly has laid her eggs, her life is over. Only a few of the caterpillars that emerge from eggs, often hidden on the underside of leaves, survive. They are eaten by birds, other insects and small animals. Caterpillars that escape grow rapidly, shedding their skins five times to permit more growth. This is unlike the young of animals with an internal skeleton, whose skin grows and stretches as the body grows.

The caterpillar has eight pairs of legs, but only the first three pairs become the legs of the adult butterfly. As the caterpillar grows it changes in appearance, becoming less inviting and, because of an odor, even repulsive to predators. On page 11, the caterpillar seems to have horns, but they serve no function except to appear threatening.

The chrysalis stage can be a matter of days or months, depending on temperature. Inside the hard shell changes take place that completely alter the body, and a full-grown butterfly emerges. On its head are two slender antennae, two large compound eyes and a long tonguelike tube for sucking nectar from flowers. Almost invisible scales, brightly colored, cover the butterfly's wings and provide the distinctive pattern another butterfly of the same kind can identify. This, of course, is necessary for successful mating.